Contents

KV-374-735

Read this first

The purpose of this book is to introduce the techniques of carving, building and modelling. From the time when Man first began to use tools to shape his flint weapons, he has carved images of the animals around him and moulded statues of the gods he worshipped out of the various materials he could find.

The ideas suggested and described here are intended to fire your imagination so that once the basic techniques have been mastered you can go on to experiment.

About plaster
Plaster is cheap and easy to work with, so if the first few efforts are not very successful — try again! Two basic kinds of plaster have been used in this book:
1. Plaster of Paris. This can be bought from hardware and do-it-yourself stores. When mixed with water it begins to harden in two or three minutes.
2. Fine grain wall filler (spackle). This again can be bought from hardware and do-it-yourself stores and is sold under various brand names, so ask the store-keeper for the right one. It is made from plaster with various additives so that it sets more slowly and will stay soft and work-able for nearly an hour.

As some ideas work better with a particular type of plaster, the correct one will be listed at the top of each idea.

Mixing plaster
1. Before you begin to mix the plaster, make sure that you have all the things you will need and that you know what you are going to do. Once the plaster starts to set you won't have much time to stop and think!
2. Measure the water into an old china or plastic bowl and add the plaster, stirring well with a metal spoon to make a smooth mixture. You will need about one spoonful of water to two spoonfuls of plaster to make a creamy mixture. The amount of mixture you will need will depend on what you are making but it is better to mix up too much than too little.

4

Model Ideas

The ideas in this book were contributed by
Rita Davies
Philip Freeman Sayer
Eileen Geipel
Alan Lewis
A. R. Philpott
Mary Seyd

Evans Brothers Limited

Published by Evans Brothers Limited
Montague House, Russell Square,
London, WC1B 5BX

Set in 12 on 13 point Photina by Filmtype Services Limited, Scarborough
and printed in Great Britain by Sackville Press Billericay Ltd, Essex

ISBN 0 237 44977 3   PRA 6579

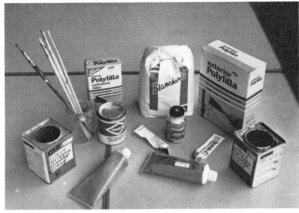

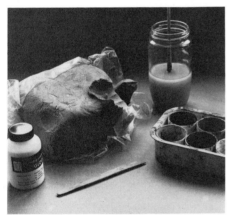

Because all plaster sets very hard, and plaster of Paris sets very quickly, there are three important things to remember:
1. Clean the bowls and spoons *as soon as you can*, if possible while the plaster is still wet. Scrape as much of the unset plaster as possible into newspaper and leave it to set before throwing it away. Then wash the bowls and spoons in lots of water.
2. If you forget to clean up immediately and the plaster goes hard in the bowl and on the spoon, leave them to soak in hot water. The plaster can then be chipped off into newspaper and thrown away.
3. *Never* put wet or dried plaster down the sink or lavatory as it may clog up the drains.

Modelling with clay
It is important when using clay to keep the material in good condition, so always keep it sealed up tightly in a plastic bag and save any spare bits left over in a separate bag, sprinkled with a little water, to stop them drying out.

5

Here is a basic kit of equipment which you will need for most of the ideas which use clay:

1. Newspaper – to cover the table and surrounding area.
2. Modelling tool – this can easily be made from an old ruler.
3. Paints – any type will do, although water colours may be inclined to smear.
4. Brush – one of the soft-hair type.
5. Water pot or jar.
6. Sponge.
7. Cellophane tape.
8. Modelling clay.
9. Varnish – this is sold under various names and can be obtained from an art supplier, hardware shop or do-it-yourself shop.

Types of wire
Modelling wire can be bought from hardware or hobby supply stores in various thicknesses and varieties. Choose a flexible type which can easily be bent but

Each of these models was made from just a small ball of clay, shaped and painted to form a hedgehog, a spider and a pig respectively. The spider's legs are made of four pipe cleaners, cut in half and bent at an angle.

The picture opposite shows two insects made from clay, with crinkled modelling wire used for the legs and wings. They have been painted in bright insect colours.

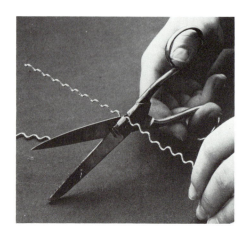

6

not so thin that it will break. The best kind is galvanized to prevent it rusting and it can be either straight or crinkled as in the picture of insects on this page.

If you have no wire cutters, you can easily make a pair by cutting a small slot in the bottom of each blade of an old pair of scissors, just below the screw that holds the blades together, using a hacksaw (see the picture opposite).

Building and carving
Any tool sharp enough to cut through wood or stone can cut you just as easily, so always use these instruments with care, and store them in a safe place when not in use. Always make sure the work is held firmly in place when working, if possible

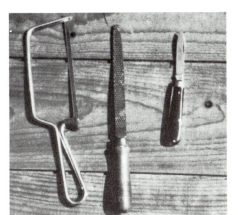

using a clamp so that both hands are free to hold the tool. When using a knife, always cut away from you, and never cut off too much at once as the tool may bend or break. Carve off small amounts bit by bit.

The basic tools for building and carving the ideas in this book need not be expensive — a junior hacksaw, a penknife and a rasp (or metal file) are all you need to start, with some fine sandpaper to finish off the work.

Before starting any of the models shown in this book, read through the instructions carefully and collect together the materials and equipment you will need. When using clay or plaster for the first time it is a good idea to begin with some small simple models, and with carving it is useful to learn how best to use the tools to achieve the effect you want.

Work on a clear surface covered with newspaper, and wear an apron or an old shirt as plaster, in particular, can be wet and messy. A large sheet of newspaper, with a hole cut in the centre for your head and a piece of string tied round the waist as a belt, works very well, if you can find nothing else.

Once you know how to use the materials and equipment described in this book, there is no limit to what you can make. You can get ideas from illustrations in books, or from actual statues or models on display in museums, art galleries and parks.

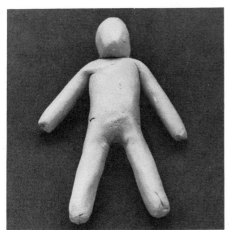

Little figures

This is a very simple way of making models of people and animals, using just the basic kit.

Collect
The basic kit (page 6).

How to start
1. Roll two 'sausages' of clay, one thicker than the other.
2. Roll another 'sausage', half as long and twice as thick. Lay the first two at each end of the thick one to form a letter 'H' and join up by moulding the clay.
3. Add a ball of clay for the head where the body joins the arms.
4. Make all the joints strong — use a damp sponge if the clay is too dry.
5. Bend the arms down and pinch the ends to make hands.
6. Bend the legs down and turn up the ends to make feet.

Now experiment
Once the basic figure is complete, any number of details can be added to make it distinctive and interesting. Add two big clay boots so that it will stand up on its own. Make an apron or skirt from a very thin layer of clay. Add buttons of clay down the front to make a shirt and drape thin strips of clay over the shoulders as braces, or around the waist as a belt.

Figures can be made to sit down as well by bending the clay legs carefully before they dry. Make a base for the figure to sit on from a small box, a piece of wood, or even perhaps a good-sized stone. Give the model a coat of paint, picking out the various features of the face and clothing, then cover it with a coat of varnish.

The techniques of creating figures of animals and people have been combined to create the model of Old Uncle Tom Cobbley and All shown on the opposite page.

Little animals

Making animal models is very similar in method to making the little figures in the last idea. Again, all that is needed is the basic kit and some imagination.

How to start
1. Roll two 'sausages' of clay of equal thickness.
2. Roll a short, extra thick piece for the body.
3. Join the first two sausages of clay, one to each end of the short, thick one, to form the shape of an H.
4. Add a good-sized piece of clay to one end for the head.
5. Make all the joints strong, using a damp sponge if the clay is too dry.
6. Bend all four legs down and bend the neck and head into position.

Now experiment

Try bending the finished animal into all sorts of different positions. Lay it on its side, sit it up like a cat or stand it up like a horse.

Improve the modelling so that it looks like a particular animal, giving its face features and adding ears and a tail. If you are making a horse, sit a little man on its back or try making more unusual animals such as a hippo or even a giraffe.

Paint the finished model in bright colours and then give it a coat of varnish.

Glove puppets

A third idea using the basic kit requires only the addition of a handkerchief to make a glove puppet, which can then be painted and dressed to look like any character you choose.

How to start

1. Take a piece of clay a bit larger than a golf ball.
2. Roll it into a ball.
3. Press it on to your first finger, maintaining its ball shape.
4. Poke in a hollow for each eye and one for the mouth.
5. Pinch out a nose.
6. Use the point of a pencil to mark details on the face.
7. Put the head in a warm place to dry.
8. Paint the hair and face.

Put the head back on your finger, wrap a handkerchief around your hand and, using your best ventriloquist voice, make the puppet speak. If you move your thumb and middle finger, the puppet can make gestures.

Now experiment
Make heads for other characters and then make more permanent gloves for them from spare pieces of fabric. Collect a variety of materials such as feathers, string, raffia and cotton wool to make hair and beards, and add hats or crowns.

Put on a puppet show, using a cardboard box with a hole cut through the top as a stage.

Models from a large ball of clay

A simple ball of clay can be made into as many things as your imagination can create — animals, insects, birds, fishes and any number of other everyday or unusual things.

Collect
Crinkled modelling wire (see page 6)
Wire cutters
Basic kit

How to start
1. Screw a double sheet of newspaper into a ball as tightly as possible.
2. Make several flat discs of clay.

13

3. Cover the paper ball with the clay and smear the joints together.
4. Make the ball smooth and strong by beating it with a ruler or a stick.

This is the basis for many different kinds of models.

The gloves for these puppets are made by cutting two identical shapes for the body and arms and stitching them together, leaving the bottom open so you can slide your hand in, and a small hole for the head. The cloak for the puppet on the left is simply a triangular piece of fabric pinned at the front.

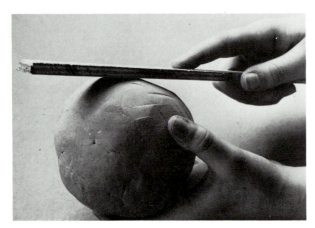

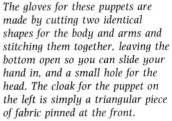

Choose attractively coloured and patterned pebbles to use as models. Your clay 'pebbles' would make good presents as they are excellent paperweights.

Start with the spider. The legs are made of eight pieces of crinkled wire which have been bent and stuck into place. Roll two little balls for eyes and stick them into place with a little moisture. Mark a pattern on its back and, when it is dry, paint it.

To make the fish, beat the body a little flatter, then cut out the fins and tail from a slab of clay and join them to the body, using the sponge.

A bird will need an extra ball for its head. Join it to the body with a thin coil of clay round its neck. Cut out wings and a tail and smear them into place. Paint or mark on feathers.

Pebbles

Stones and pebbles from the garden, the park or the seashore can be found in an infinite variety of shapes, sizes, colours and textures. Here is a way of using the method described in the previous idea to make replicas of the more interesting and attractive pebbles you find.

Collect
Three or four pebbles
A sprayer
Basic kit

How to start
1. Make a ball of clay around a piece of newspaper as described in the preceding idea.
2. Choose a pebble, then beat the ball of clay into shape to resemble it as closely as possible in both shape and size.
3. Texture the surface of the clay to match the pebble.
4. Allow it to dry.
5. Apply paint to get the right effect; stipple, spray, sponge, or use any other method you can think of to obtain the best results.

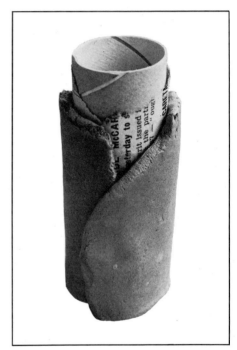

Now experiment
Arrange a group of pebbles in an attractive formation. Design pebbles from memory or imagination and use them as a background for some of your other models.

A candelight tree

Collect
A short cardboard tube (toilet paper tube)
A small candle   A penknife
Basic kit (page 6)

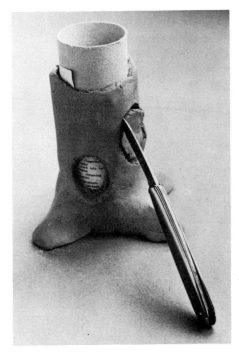

How to start
1. Wrap a piece of newspaper round the tube and stick it in place with cellophane tape.
2. Roll a piece of clay out flat and wrap it round the tube.
3. Smear the join together. Trim off the bottom with a penknife to make it level.
4. Model three of four 'roots' to stick out a little way and help the tree stand firmly.
5. Cut several large holes in the sides of the clay tube.
6. Slide the cardboard tube and newspaper out of the tree and let the clay stiffen a little.
7. Finish off the modelling.
8. Paint the inside of the tree using a pale colour, then paint the outside using darker, reddish brown.
9. Put the candle in a saucer, place the tree over the top and light it carefully through one of the holes.

Now experiment
Using the same basic shape for the inside, try texturing the outside of the tree to look like bark. Make a clay dish for the tree to stand in — this could be painted green to resemble grass, with perhaps a few flowers, and even clay insects.

17

The effect of the candlelight flickering against the pale yellow inside of the tree is very attractive, particularly in a darkened room.

In the flower-pot jar opposite, the semi-circular join of the clay has been made part of the pattern. If you want to use it as a flower vase, replace the jar after you have removed the cardboard and fill it with water for your flowers.

A flower~pot jar

Another way of making something both useful and attractive uses a similar technique to the previous idea, but this time a glass jar or a plastic pot is used to mould the clay round.

How to start
1. Wrap a piece of corrugated cardboard around the jar and stick it in place with cellophane tape.
2. Roll out on a piece of cloth sufficient clay to cover the corrugated cardboard. The clay should be about 15mm thick.
3. Wrap the clay around the corrugated cardboard and join it together, either by moulding the two edges together or, if

Collect
A glass jar or plastic pot
A cloth
A sheet of light corrugated cardboard
Basic kit (page 6)

they are neat and clean-cut, by overlapping them and rounding the top edge smoothly.
4. Press a pattern into the clay with the end of a pencil or an apple-corer, following the edges around.
5. Allow the clay to dry.
6. Slide out the jar and dispose of the corrugated cardboard.
7. To paint the pot, try spraying paint on with an aerosol spray.
8. Coat the finished pot with varnish.

Now experiment
The shape of the jar decides what shape the pot will be, so collect some unusual-shaped jars and try using more adventurous patterns and colours.

With experience you can pattern the clay before it goes around the jar, but don't forget the corrugated cardboard or the clay will crack as it shrinks.

Bottle shapes

Bottles are just as useful as jars, and some very convincing shapes of people can be modelled on them, using soft putty.

How to start
1. Mix up the wallpaper paste as described on page 65. Tear the newspaper into strips and paste them all around the bottle. Let the paper dry.
2. Shape a head from a lump of putty on to the neck of the bottle, pulling out a piece to form a nose, pushing in two holes for the eyes and making all the features of a character's face.
3. Cover the head with strips of pasted paper and make sure that all the layers are glued down really well before adding a final layer or two of tissue paper.
4. Paint the head and the bottle itself.
5. Add arms made from pieces of thin cardboard attached to the back and bent round the bottle.

Now experiment
You could make an army of soldiers with different bottles, or figures wearing national costumes of different countries. Try making a Red Indian with small feathers around his head and a tomahawk in his hand.

Collect
Some interestingly-shaped bottles
Soft modelling putty
Wallpaper paste
Newspaper
Tissue paper
Poster paints
Coloured paper and thin cardboard
Scraps of material

20

Plaster paperweight

Here is a way of using plaster to make very good gifts and colourful ornaments.

Collect
Plastic bag
Small piece of felt
Scissors
Chalk or a ball-point pen
Glue
Clear varnish
Poster or powdered paints and brushes
Plaster of Paris
Water
Mixing bowl and tablespoon

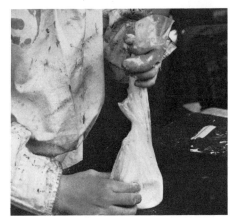

How to start
1. Put four tablespoonfuls of water into a bowl and add eight level tablespoonfuls of plaster of Paris.
2. Stir well and then pour the mixture into the corner of a plastic bag.
3. Twist the top of the bag above the plaster and place on a table for about two minutes until the plaster begins to set.
4. Now twist the bag and the plaster into a strange shape, holding it in place until the plaster is firm enough to keep its shape.
5. Leave the bag for about half an hour to set completely before removing it.
6. What does the shape resemble? A monster, some strange creature from the sea, a face? Paint it in bright colours and varnish it.

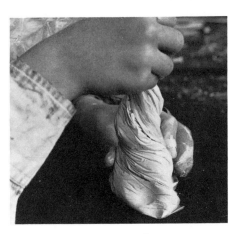

21

This fierce soldier was made from a short, squat bottle. You could make a knight in shining armour by wrapping a piece of cooking foil round the body of the bottle and making a cardboard sword and shield covered with foil sweet wrapping. A scrap of shiny fabric would make him a splendid cloak.

The paperweight on the left was made by twisting the bag with the plaster in it. The one on the right was made by modelling the plaster in the bag.

It is a good idea to stick some felt to the base of the paperweight so that it does not scratch the furniture. Place the model on the felt and draw round it with some chalk or a pen. Cut out the shape and glue it firmly to the base.

Plaster blocks

Collect
Small square supermarket trays
Modelling putty
Clear varnish
Poster or powdered paints and brushes
Plaster of Paris
Water
Mixing bowl and tablespoon

There are two kinds of blocks — relief and intaglio. A relief block is one where the design stands up from the surface, whereas an intaglio block is the complete opposite, the design being cut into the surface of the plaster. Both types can be made to look very attractive when painted in a variety of colours.

How to make a relief block
1. Take a square tray and make a bed of smooth modelling putty at the bottom.
2. Make dents and hollows in the putty

24

by carving pieces out, and pressing objects into it, to make a good design.

3. Put seven tablespoonfuls of water into a bowl and add fourteen level tablespoonfuls of plaster of Paris.

4. Mix together and then pour the plaster into the tray.

5. Allow to set (about an hour) and then carefully remove the block from its base.

As this is a relief block the pattern or design should stand up and be easy to feel with the fingertips.

How to make an intaglio block

1. Make a bed of smooth modelling putty in the bottom of another tray.

2. Model the surface, adding little pieces of putty so that the design stands up from the surface.

3. Mix up the same amount of plaster of Paris as before and pour it into the tray. Remove the block when the plaster is hard.

This intaglio block is different from the first in that the design is set into the plaster.

Now experiment

Try making a large picture or design in a box lid using both relief and intaglio shapes, or make a row of blocks with a different animal or bird on each one.

See the different effects you can get by using plastic food containers (or, as in the pictures, the inside of a chocolate box) as moulds, instead of putty.

25

Two of these blocks are relief blocks and two are intaglio. Can you tell which are which?

The picture opposite shows two sand relief blocks. One has been painted to bring out the pattern, and one has been left plain.

Sand relief blocks

Making a sand relief block requires more careful preparation and will take longer. The most important thing is patience. Don't spoil everything by rushing.

Collect
A shoe box
Four cupfuls of sand
Vaseline
Cellophane tape
A small stone or pebble
Plaster of Paris
Water
Mixing bowls and a cup

How to start

1. Slit three corners of the shoe box so that the edges flap down, then join them together again with cellophane tape.

2. Grease the inside walls of the box well with Vaseline.

3. Put the sand into a bowl and mix in a cupful of water until it is just damp enough to hold the shape of the pattern drawn into it.

4. Press the wet sand into the bottom of the box.

27

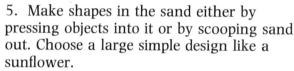

5. Make shapes in the sand either by pressing objects into it or by scooping sand out. Choose a large simple design like a sunflower.

6. Small objects can be pressed into the sand as well. This flower has a small stone pressed into its middle.

7. Mix two cupfuls of water with four cupfuls of plaster of Paris and pour the mixture into the box very carefully without disturbing the sand.

8. Let the plaster dry overnight before removing the cellophane tape from the corners of the box.

9. Bend down the sides and carefully remove the plaster block. Some of the sand will have stuck to the plaster, but this can be lightly brushed off.

Now experiment

Make a labyrinth. Starting in the centre, cut a circular groove in the sand round and round in bigger and bigger circles (always leaving a good space between each groove) until you finally come to the edge. Prepare the block in the usual way

and when it is finished, place a glass marble in the groove and tilt the block backward and forward.

Carving a plaster block

Collect
A cardboard box
Poster or powdered paints and brushes
A sheet of plastic
Plaster of Paris
Water
Linoleum cutting tool or penknife
Mixing bowl and cup

How to start
1. Line the box with the sheet of plastic. Make sure it covers the sides.
2. Put three cupfuls of water into a bowl and add six cupfuls of plaster of Paris. Stir well.
3. Pour the mixture into the lined box and let it set hard.
4. Remove the block from the box and scratch a design into the surface. Scrape away parts of the block, leaving the design in relief.
5. Paint the block in bright colours, varnish it.

Now experiment
Use a cardboard tube with a piece of plastic fixed firmly across one end. Pour the plaster into the tube. When it has set, remove the cardboard tube and carve the plaster into a statuette or figurine.

On this plaster block, the face has been carved away below
the background, and then painted brightly.

This tubular plaster block has been carved
with faces on all sides like a totem pole.

Sand and wall filler carving

If you make a block of sand and wall filler instead of plaster, you will find that its quality and texture are very similar to those of natural stone.

Collect
Sand   Chalk
Wall filler (spackle)
Cardboard box
Large bowl
Stick   Water
Hacksaw   Rasp

How to start
1. Mix equal amounts of builder's sand and wall filler in the bowl. (Take care not to use sand taken from private land.)
2. Add water gradually, stirring all the time, until you have a stiff paste.
3. Pour the mixture into the cardboard box and let it set overnight.
4. Remove the box, and the 'stone' block is ready to carve, using the same techniques as for carving plaster.

You can see from this carved sand and wall filler block that its texture and effect are very similar to those of limestone.

31

Wall filler and boxes

Any model which does not obviously represent a recognisable figure such as a person, an animal or a building, can be described as an 'abstract'. Here is an idea for creating abstract models using old cardboard boxes covered with wall filler.

Collect
Empty boxes, plastic containers, etc.
Glue
Wall filler (spackle)
Plastic bowl and a piece of wood
Stout cardboard or wood for a base

How to start
1. Build an abstract model on the base, using the boxes. Stick them together to make an interesting shape.
2. Mix a quantity of wall filler in the plastic bowl. Put a quantity of water in the bowl and sprinkle the wall filler on to the surface, stirring the mixture with a stick. Keep stirring until it becomes creamy and thick.
3. Pour the mixture carefully over the model, scooping it out of the bowl with a spoon or with your hand, and spreading it where necessary.
4. Mix up some more wall filler if there is not enough to cover the model.

Now experiment
Try making different effects on the surface of the model, using a blunt knife or your fingers.

Plaster and modelling putty

Collect
Modelling putty
Egg cartons
Poster or powdered paints and brushes
A piece of cardboard
Glue
Wall filler (spackle)
Water
Mixing bowl and tablespoon

How to start
1. Model some penguins from the putty.
2. Put five tablespoonfuls of water into a bowl and add ten level tablespoonfuls of wall filler. Mix well.
3. Using your fingers or a spoon, coat the models with the wall filler and allow to set.
4. Arrange small pieces of egg box on the cardboard and glue them in place.
5. Coat the egg boxes with the wall filler mixture to make them look like rocks and allow to set.
6. When they are dry, paint the penguins and the rocks.

Now experiment
Using egg cartons as a base, model the landscape of a distant planet. The strange creatures living on the planet can be modelled in putty and covered with wall filler as above. Why not even make a space craft from a ball of clay, with wire legs for landing?

Houses and buildings

The painted penguins show up well against the snowy rocks of their background. What other figures could you add to this Arctic scene?

This idea shows how to make complicated and interesting structures, such as houses, using cardboard.

Collect
Any empty cardboard boxes, tubes, etc.
Matchboxes, cocktail sticks, toothpicks
Coloured gummed paper
Corrugated cardboard or paper
Scissors
Paint brush
Cellophane tape
White glue (such as Elmer's or P.V.A.)
Thickly mixed powdered paints

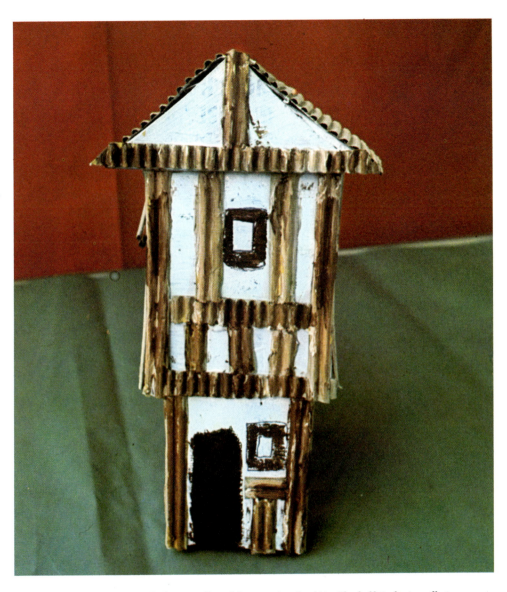

This medieval house was made from cardboard boxes painted white. The half-timbering effect was obtained by painting strips of corrugated cardboard the colours of old smokey wooden beams and gluing them into place.

How to start

Medieval houses had one or two upper storeys overhanging the ground floor. Find three boxes of different sizes which will do this when placed one on top of the other. Make sure that the base is firm and will not topple over.

1. Glue the boxes together.
2. Choose a box for the roof which has a base large enough to fit over the top box of the house.
3. Laying the box flat, place a ruler across the box, half-way along the longest side, and draw a line (Fig. 1). Use a sharp pair of scissors to cut the box in two.
4. Starting at the centre of the newly-cut edge, cut down into the corners to leave two large central triangles (Fig. 2). Bend the sides in, folding the flaps in between the triangles and attach them with cellophane tape (Fig. 3).
5. Glue the roof on to the rest of the building.
6. With the corrugated side of a piece of corrugated paper face up, cut a piece to cover the roof and glue it in position.

7. Paint the roof brown and the rest of the house white. Use a thick creamy mixture of paint in order to cover the writing on the boxes.
8. Add strips of corrugated paper to represent the old wooden beams and paint these as well.
9. Add doors and windows using gummed paper. If you are making a street of houses try adding a shop sign to one of the houses with some paper hanging from a toothpick or cocktail stick.

Now experiment
Make a complete medieval street scene
with some modelled people in the streets.
A book with pictures of the period will
provide some ideas.

Back to the present day, and why not
design a school building, or a church, or
the houses in a street nearby?

Try looking into the future as well, and
make an imaginary space-age town, with
robots and spaceships made from balls of
clay, as described on page 13. Empty
plastic bottles or yoghurt containers are
ideal for this.

Making a
model village

Another way of making houses, churches,
shops and other buildings, is to add wall
filler to the cardboard boxes used in the
last idea. This will give the effect of the
plaster used on real houses. All kinds of
extra details can be added to make a
realistic village scene, including real
leaves, twigs, dried flowers and models of
people and small animals.

Collect
Boxes, tubes and cartons of all sizes
A large sheet of plywood
Poster or powdered paints and brushes
Some twigs, leaves and dried flowers
Wall filler (spackle)
Water
Mixing bowl and tablespoon

37

How to start

A medieval street.

1. Choose several boxes of different sizes for houses, cottages, a church and shops. Make roofs out of folded cardboard adding small tubes of cardboard for chimneys.

2. Mix the wall filler to an even consistency and cover the buildings with a layer, using your fingers to smooth it on. Leave the buildings to dry.

3. Paint them carefully, adding details such as doors and windows.

4. Cover the plywood with a layer of wall filler and set the houses into it. While the mixture is still wet, add the twigs and

Above is a scene of a village street. Plenty of realistic detail can be added to it.

leaves for trees and bushes.
The village pond can be made from a piece of foil and the road through the village by sprinkling fine gravel or sand.
5. When the base is dry, paint in the grass and sprinkle some more gravel and a few pebbles for realism.

Now experiment
Make model cars from matchboxes covered with wall filler and shaped while the filler is still moist. Add buttons for wheels.

Try modelling part of the village or town centre where you live.

Models made with wire

Wire can be used to mould the basic shapes for intricate models using plaster or wall filler. The wire helps strengthen the plaster so that very unusual and realistic shapes can be made, particularly of insects.

This first model is of an octopus — an ideal shape because the wire is just right for the octopus's long legs.

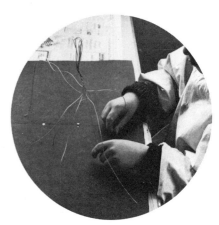

Collect
Modelling wire (straight)
Wire cutters
Newspaper
Wallpaper paste
Poster or powdered paints and brushes
Wall filler (spackle)
Water
Bowls
Teaspoon and tablespoon

How to start
1. Pour 4 cups of water into a bowl and sprinkle three teaspoonfuls of wallpaper paste into it. Stir well and let it stand for fifteen minutes.
2. Cut the wire into four equal lengths.
3. Bend each piece of wire in half and then twist them all together at the top to make a head and body.
4. Bend out the legs all round.

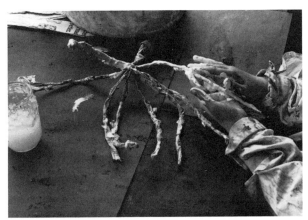

5. Tear some newspaper into strips.

6. Dip the strips of paper into the paste and then wind them round the wire shape to form the head, body and each separate leg. When the legs and body are quite thick leave it to dry. Make sure at this stage that your octopus is standing in a good position with all the legs bent in the right direction as it is difficult to change it once the paper has dried.

7. Put six tablespoonfuls of water into a bowl and add twelve level tablespoonfuls of wall filler.

8. Stir well and then cover the model with a layer of the mixture, dabbing and smoothing it with your fingers.

9. Leave it to set and then paint it.

Now experiment
Animals, trees and plants can all be made in this way. Try making a jungle with all sorts of wild animals, insects such as spiders, snakes and strange plants.

Here is a very jolly octopus made from wire and newspaper strips. You should always wait until the model is completely dry before painting it.

More models with wire

Modelling wire can be crinkled as well as straight and the crinkled type is ideal for making insects.

Collect
Modelling wire (crinkled)
Wire cutters
Basic kit (page 6)

How to start
1. Look closely at a wasp, then shape a piece of clay into a 'carrot' for the abdomen.
2. Make a thorax and a small ball for the head.
3. Cut seven equal pieces of crinkled wire twisting one piece through the three parts of the clay body to join them together. Then, turning the wasp upside down, add the remaining six pieces of wire to the underside of the thorax to form legs.
4. Bend two long lengths of wire round, to form ovals for the wings, and stick them into either side of the thorax, above the legs.
5. Allow the clay to dry.
6. Make a bend in each leg and then cut them to equal

Above. Three little dolls made from fabric over a wire-netting frame.
Below. You can bend the wire into different positions to give life to your models.

lengths so that the wasp stands firmly.
7. Paint it in bright clean colours and
finish with a final coat of varnish.

Now experiment
There are a great many other insects to be
made in this way, including butterflies and
moths, using paper for their wings.

People and animals are equally simple to
make using a small marble-sized ball of
clay for the body and smaller balls for the
head, hands and feet. Use crinkled wire for
the arms and legs, and the tail if you are
making an animal, and paint the finished
model when it has dried.

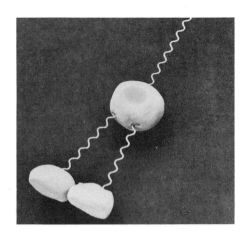

Plaster and fabric models

Odd pieces of material can be combined
with plaster to form models of people in
different costumes.

Collect
A square piece of wire netting
Powdered or poster paints and brushes
Modelling wire (straight)
Wire cutters
Oddments of fabric
Wall filler (spackle)
Water
Mixing bowl and tablespoon

How to start
1. Curl the wire netting round to make

44

a tube, then crush the top to make a roughly-shaped cone.

2. Cut a length of wire and wind it tightly round the cone near the top, leaving the two ends sticking out for arms.

3. Put twelve tablespoonfuls of water into a bowl and add eighteen level tablespoonfuls of wall filler to make a thin mixture.

4. Cut or tear the material into strips and dip them into the mixture.

5. Starting with the head, wind strips of material round the wire frame until you get a good shape.

6. Continue to cover the wire shape, using larger pieces of fabric to drape over the arms.

7. Add details such as string or fur for hair, buttons or sequins to decorate the clothes.

8. Paint the model when it is dry, adding patterns on the dress if need be.

Now experiment
Try making a group of figures, a rock group, some historical characters or dolls in national costume.

Collect any pieces of gold string and silver paper to make into necklaces and crowns for a king and queen. Why not make a throne for each, using a small cardboard box? Cut the back of the throne from a sheet of cardboard, making it the same width as the box, and glue it on. It can then be painted and decorated with anything you can find to befit a king and queen.

This very realistic crocodile was made using fabric and paste on a wire-netting base. It is an ideal technique for making large-scale models such as this one.

The animal on the right is made of wire, paper and plaster. If it needs strengthening, try using strips of fabric dipped in plaster and wound on to the framework.

Wire, paper and plaster

You can now make a procession of animals to go with the king and queen.

Collect
Wire netting
Wire cutters
Strips of cloth or bandage
Plaster of Paris
Wallpaper paste
Newspaper
Paints
Brush
Varnish (not essential)

How to start
1. Cut the wire netting carefully into two pieces, one of rectangular shape and the other a smaller square.

2. Shape the larger piece into a head and body by squeezing the wire into shape. Then cut the second piece into two strips to make the legs.

3. Attach the legs by twisting them right around the body and then finish squeezing the body into shape.

4. Mix a jar of wallpaper paste and, while it thickens, cut some strips of newspaper. Brush the paste on both sides of the paper strips, then lay them, over-lapping, one at a time, on the wire frame. Leave it overnight to dry.

5. If you want to make the animal more solid, cover it with strips of cloth which have been soaked in plaster of Paris. Remember that plaster dries very fast so work quickly, squeezing the model into shape as you go.

6. When dry, paint with poster colours and finally add a coat of clear varnish.

Pipe cleaner, straw and putty models

On page 32 we showed how to make abstract models using boxes and wall filler. The next few ideas suggest ways of using all sorts of materials to create abstracts. The first one uses pipe cleaners and drinking straws.

Collect
Modelling clay or putty
Pipe cleaners
Drinking straws
Gold or silver spray paint

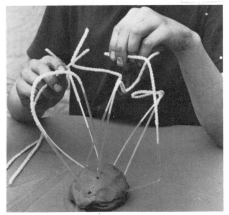

How to start

1. Make a firm clay or putty base for the model. This can be a rectangular or triangular shape, or a ball with a flat base.
2. Push a few straws into the base from a number of different angles.
3. Join the straws together with pipe cleaners, feeding them into the ends of the straws, and building up the shape with curves and straight lines. Make longer connections with pipe cleaners and straws joined together.
4. Place the finished model on some sheets of newspaper and spray all over with a gold or silver spray paint.

Now experiment

Instead of one main base, try making a start using several bases, or turn the model into a mobile to hang from the ceiling on a thin wire or string.

Thin, coloured fuse wire, or the type of wire used in the garden, is useful for connecting the straws.

Instead of spraying the model, use water-based house paint (emulsion paint) in several bright colours.

Wire sculptures

A similar but more intricate effect can be made using fairly thin wire in the same way as the straws and pipe cleaners were modelled in the last idea. Try using coloured electrical wire for variety.

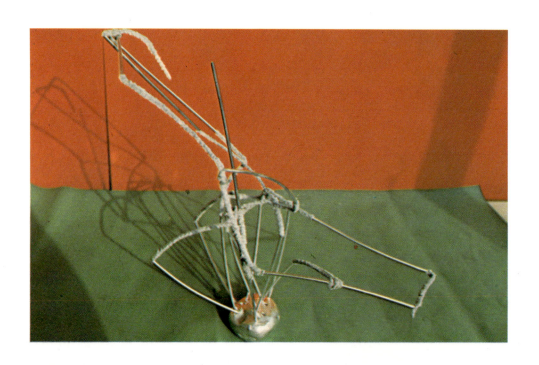

50

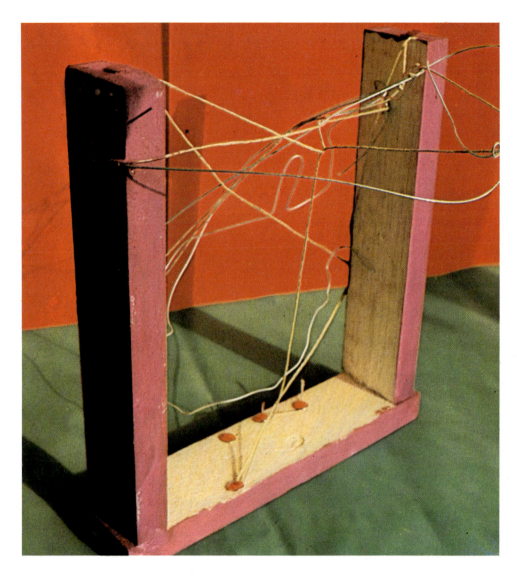

Three abstracts made with wire. Because wire can be bent and twisted in any direction it is an excellent material to make abstract models with.

Collect

Wire of different thicknesses
Modelling clay or putty
Paints
Brush
Scissors or wire cutters
Newspaper
Wallpaper paste

How to start

1. Mould a circular or square base from clay or putty. Cover it with strips of newspaper pasted across each other and let it dry before painting it.
2. Build up an abstract wire sculpture by pushing separate lengths into the base. Twist and shape them, joining pieces together to make a model which is pleasing to look at from all angles. Use just one kind of wire to start with and then try adding different thicknesses and colours.

Now experiment

Make a coiled abstract, pushing the wire into the base and building up twisted and coiled shapes very close together. Try using twisted and coiled pipe cleaners to join the pieces of wire.

Make a symmetrical sculpture by bending each piece of wire at the same point so that the pattern looks the same whichever side you view it from. See how complex a symmetrical sculpture you can make.

Paint or spray paint the finished model. A silver or gold spray paint gives an effective result.

Using wire, string and wood

This idea is really a combination of some of the suggestions already described. Experiment as much as possible, building an abstract model that is pleasing to look at.

Collect
Ball of string
Some solid pieces of balsa wood
Thin wire
Coloured drawing pins or nails
White glue (such as Elmer's or P.V.A.)

How to start
1. Make a solid base with three pieces of balsa wood, one flat and two upright. Glue them together.
2. Cut different lengths of string and wire. Pin them to the wood at one side, stretch them across, pulling the string taut, and attach them to the other pieces of wood. Bend the wire at different angles and intertwine the string around and through.
3. Use the coloured pins as part of the design so that they make patterns on the wood. If they look clumsy, use tiny nails which do not show as much.

Now experiment
Try placing the pieces of wood at different angles, having only one upright and two flat pieces or perhaps several uprights.

Be very critical of your abstracts, and try designing them on paper first. As you build, watch the spaces made between and around the sections so that you create a balanced pattern. Look carefully at your finished model and see if the shape suggests an idea or title to your mind.

The abstract above was made with cardboard boxes covered in wall filler (see page 32). You can make different textures on the surface before the wall filler sets. The model on the right is made from pieces of wood.

Wood abstracts

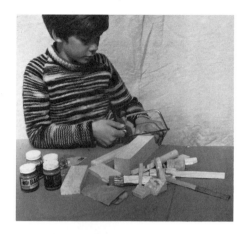

Collect
Offcuts and scraps of wood of all kinds
including, if possible, some balsa wood
Glue or wood adhesive
Gold or silver spray paint or ordinary
gloss paint
Turpentine   Saw
Craft knife   Sandpaper

How to start
1. Find a solid piece of wood to use as a
base and a number of smaller pieces to
fit together.
2. Build up a shape by gluing the pieces
together. Before gluing down the
individual pieces, sandpaper all the rough
edges.
3. When it is finished, decide how it
should be decorated, either by spraying it
with gold or silver paint, or by painting it
several different colours with gloss paint.

Now experiment
Create a model with tiny strips of wood,
particularly with balsa which is so easy to
cut, building the model up piece by piece
until it exactly represents the abstract you
have imagined.

String shapes

You can use knotted and woven string to
create interesting abstracts.

Collect
Wallpaper paste
Vaseline or cooking oil
Balloons and polythene bags
Tissue paper   Sisal or jute string

How to start
1. Make up the wallpaper paste in a bowl.
2. Blow up a balloon or fill a polythene bag with water. Tie the ends. Smear the balloon with Vaseline or oil so that the string will not stick.
3. Tie several lengths of string together and dip them into the paste. Then drape them over the balloon and tie them again at the bottom. This will give you a framework to weave other pieces of string through. You can completely cover the balloon, or leave spaces like netting.
4. When the paste has dried and the string is stiff, burst the balloon.
5. You may find it easier to cover the balloon with a layer of tissue paper first. Cover this with paste, and wind the string on top.

Now experiment
Instead of paste, try using wall filler (spackle) for a different effect.

Paper cylinder shapes

Making paper cylinders and arranging them into all kinds of strange constructions is not only great fun, but requires very little preparation. Only a few tools and materials are necessary.

Above. Balloons covered with coloured string. You can leave the ends hanging down in tassels.

Right. Two models made of paper shapes. In the top picture, paper cylinders have formed a fantastic bird. The bottom construction is an abstract made from paper triangles.

58

How to start

1. Cut the paper into a series of strips of different lengths and widths. It is a good idea to decide on a colour scheme first or just use one colour. If you are using white cardboard, this can be painted later.

2. Glue each strip individually to form a cylinder. Glue is preferable but, if none is available, cellophane tape will do if used in very small pieces that will not show and spoil the look of the finished model.

3. When you have a good collection, begin joining them together — again using glue if possible or small pieces of cellophane tape. Build some lengths of cylinders and then place them one on top of the other.

Keep adding shapes on all sides of the model, making sure it is balanced and steady as it grows. Watch the spaces carefully as you attach each cylinder, varying the position and angle here and there.

4. When the model is a satisfactory shape, look at it from all angles and decide whether or not to add colour in the form of paint or coloured gummed paper. Perhaps the model could turn into a snake, an exotic bird or a fantastic dragon. On the other hand it may be just right as an abstract design in paper.

Now experiment

Add curled strips of paper to make each cylinder shape into a fabulous monster. Pull the strip of paper between your thumb and the blade of a pair of scissors to make it curl.

Collect

Sheets of firm coloured paper or thin cardboard
White glue (such as Elmer's or P.V.A.)
Cellophane tape
Coloured gummed paper (not essential)
Scissors
Paint brush
Poster and powdered paints

Eyes can be made from buttons or pieces of cardboard. Add a long, colourful tail to make it into a bird.

Build up a model from different shapes made from strips of paper. Try constructing a model from triangular shapes. Fold the strips into four pieces and then overlap and stick or staple the first piece over the last to form an open triangle.

Another model can be built with open squares or many-sided shapes made by folding and joining strips of paper. Make an abstract model which stands as tall as you are. Think carefully about the sizes to be used and where to place the largest and smallest shapes so that the whole structure will stand up.

Card slotting

Another idea using the same basic materials as for making cylinders, involves cutting slits in squares of cardboard and slotting them together. This is very simple indeed — but any number of interesting constructions can be made, adding paints of different colours for effect.

Collect
A sheet of stiff cardboard
A strong pair of scissors or craft knife
White glue (such as Elmer's or P.V.A.)
Poster or spray paints

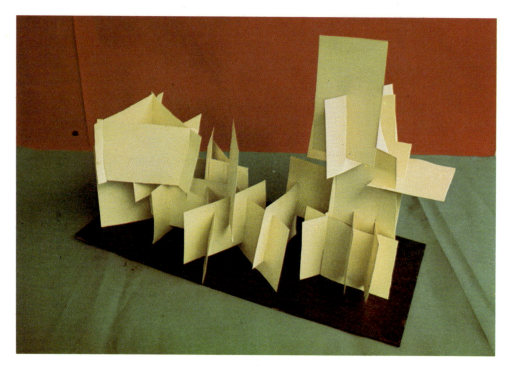

Above. This slotted card construction looks very impressive painted in only one colour. The knight on horseback opposite is cut from stiff card and bent and folded into position. Use coloured foil and gummed paper to make his armour and his horse's saddle.

How to start

1. Cut the cardboard into a number of small rectangles and squares.

2. Cut slits half-way across the middle of each one.

3. Build a structure by slotting the cards together and extending the model both horizontally and vertically.

4. Paint or spray the final model. The abstract will look very effective if you limit the colour scheme to only two colours. Try, for example, painting some of the surfaces red and leaving the others plain.

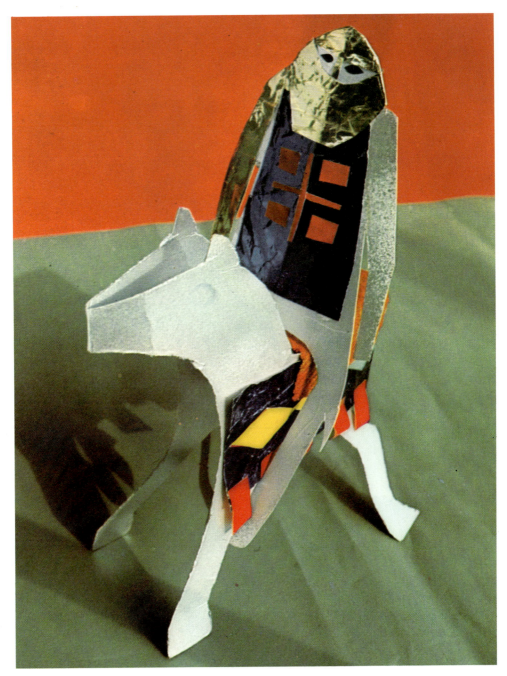

Now experiment

Thin sheets of balsa wood are ideal for slotting together. This will require a craft knife and a steel ruler. Cut the balsa wood in the same way as the cardboard, only this time cut actual 'slots' as wide as the wood is thick. Build up a model using glue where necessary. Unless the finished model is to be sprayed, it is a good idea to paint each section separately before assembly.

Using papier mâché

Papier mâché (which literally means mashed-up paper) is always fun to work with and requires no expensive ingredients — just old newspaper and some paste — but the number of things of different shapes and sizes you can make depends only on your imagination.

Before preparing the papier mâché, decide on the type of model you want to make. It could be an animal or a sculptured head, or even an abstract model on a solid base of wood or cardboard.

Collect

Newspaper
Large plastic bowl
Wallpaper paste
Water
Wooden spoon or stick
Large jar and brush
Poster paints
Varnish (not essential)

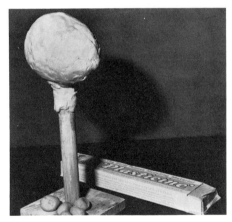

How to start

1. Tear the newspaper into very small pieces and fill the bowl until it is about half full. How much you will need will depend, of course, on the size of the model, but about sixteen double newspaper sheets to a medium-sized jar of paste is a good quantity.

2. Mix up the paste, beginning with a small amount of water and a sprinkle of paste. Keep stirring until it thickens and then add more water and another sprinkling of paste. Keep repeating the process until a creamy consistency is obtained. It will take about ten minutes.

3. Add the paste to the paper and keep stirring. The ideal method is to use your hands, but if this is too messy, use a wooden spoon. The final mixture should not be too soggy but the pieces of newspaper must be thoroughly soaked. The paste and paper must blend to make a workable mixture which can be moulded by hand without falling apart.

4. Work the papier mâché, using it, as far as possible, in one lump. Press it, squeeze it and pull it into whatever shape you have chosen to make.

5. Leave the finished model for a day or two to dry before painting it.

6. A final coat of varnish will finish it off.

Papier mâché puppets

You can use papier mâché to make very convincing heads for glove puppets. The heads are modelled first in putty.

Collect
A short length of broom handle
An offcut of wood
Modelling putty
Wallpaper paste
Tissue paper
Newspaper torn into small squares
Knife
Paints

How to start
1. Fix the broom handle into the centre of the wood square to use as a modelling stand.
2. Using marble-sized pieces of modelling putty, build up the head shape you want around the top of the post, extending the putty a short way down the post for a neck. Model the main features of the face.

Here is a papier mâché creature with a long red tongue.

66

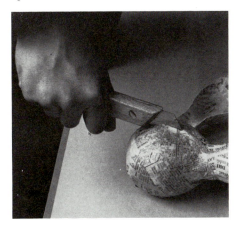

Pasting on another layer of newspaper. Using a modelling stand leaves both your hands free to model the puppet's head.

3. Cover the head with a layer of dampened tissue paper first, then a layer of paste and then a layer of newspaper pieces. Add a second layer of paste, and one of newspaper immediately. Allow to dry, then add two more layers, pressing out any bubbles or creases with your thumb as you go. Leave the head to dry hard.

4. Hold the head and base on its side as shown in the photograph, and cut with a knife from the bottom of the neck to the top of the head. Turn it over and repeat on the other side. Ease the halves off. Paste the edges to be joined and then apply paper pieces first to the top of the head, then the sides of the neck and finally all round. Add a final layer or two to the whole head and leave to dry.

5. Paint the face of the puppet and glue on

hair made from unravelled string or cotton wool. You can make your puppet a simple glove from a handkerchief wrapped round your hand, or more elaborate costumes from scraps of material.

Now experiment
To make a really large head, cover a blown-up balloon with strips of pasted paper in the same way. When the paper is dry, let the air out of the balloon and you can then work on the shell.

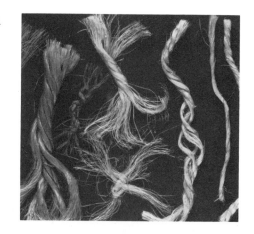

String puppets

These puppets are made entirely of string.

How to start
1. Make the body pieces out of thick string or rope cut into suitable lengths.
2. Use the fine string to bind the arms and legs on to the main body. Alternatively you can open up the fibres in the string of the main body and push the arms and legs through.
3. Make hair and beards by fraying short pieces of string, or by sewing on extra lengths.
4. Use different coloured string for the hair, clothes or decoration of your figure. You could add features such as eyes, noses and mouths with a coloured felt pen.
5. Attach thin strings to the puppet's arms and legs so that they move when you pull the strings.

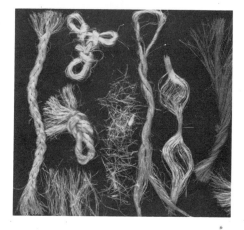

Collect
Pieces of rope or thick string
A few lengths of fine string
Paint or coloured felt pens

Papier mâché masks

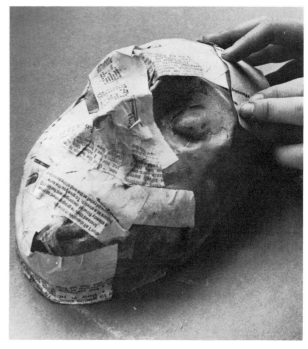

Collect
Vaseline
Wallpaper paste
A saucer of water
Basic kit

How to start
1. Use the clay to model a face about the same size as your own.
2. When it has dried a little, smear the surface lightly with Vaseline, making sure it is evenly coated all over.
3. Tear a sheet of newspaper into small square pieces and put some of these pieces into water to soften.
4. Using one cupful of water, mix up some wallpaper paste.
5. Take the pieces of paper which have been soaking in water and use them to

The Imp of Mischief; a glove puppet with a modelled head.

Right. Various string puppets. If you cannot find thick string or rope to use for the bodies of your puppets, plait or twist several lengths together to make a stronger piece.

cover the clay face. On top of this glue several more layers using the wallpaper paste. Remember to leave holes for the eyes.

6. Put the mask somewhere warm to dry out and then gently ease away the paper shell from the clay underneath.

7. Paint the inside of the mask with glue to strengthen it and let it dry out again.

8. Paint the mask in an unusual way, adding any extras such as hair, eyebrows or a beard.

Now experiment
Make masks of different characters and use them for acting plays and pantomimes.

String masks

You can make some really exciting and dramatic masks by winding great hunks of rope about and binding them into shapes. You may be able to find old bits of rope on the seashore, but check carefully that they are not oily before you take them home.

If you haven't got any rope, try binding bundles of string together. Decorate your masks with coloured pieces of string, bits of cloth, fur or feathers.

These drawings may suggest ways of beginning to make masks, and you may find other ideas if you look at tribal masks in museums.

Carving soap

The next few ideas are all concerned with carving different materials and before you begin you should read the advice on carving on page 7.

It is a good idea to start by carving a soft material, and one of the most easily available is ordinary household soap. Different coloured soaps can be used according to the object being carved.

Collect
A large bar of soap, preferably green or yellow
Penknife
Pencil
Soft cloth

How to start
1. Scratch a design on the bar of soap using the pencil. Make it simple in shape as soap is a brittle material.
2. Start to carve the shape carefully with the penknife remembering not to cut away too much at once.
3. If the carving breaks in the wrong place, it can be mended quite easily by softening the broken surfaces with a little water and pressing them together again.
4. Smooth the carving with the knife blade and polish it with a soft cloth. Soften any leftover chips of soap with warm water and squeeze them into a small bar to use again — or to wash with!

These chunky carvings were made from bars of soap. Soap is a very satisfying material to carve as you can give it a very smooth finish.

Candles

Carving a candle is very similar to carving soap. Wax is a soft material, easy to work with and, like soap, it is cheap and easily obtained. As well as carving all kinds of patterns and designs on the surface, you can also paint the candles in different colours, to make attractive presents.

Collect
Ordinary white wax candles
Sharp pencil
Penknife
Acrylic paints
Rags
Soft cloth

These carved candles would make excellent Christmas presents.

How to start

1. Grip the candle gently for a few minutes so that the warmth of your hands softens the wax slightly.

2. Scratch a pattern on the candle with a sharp pencil and then carve it with the knife. Take care as the knife can easily slip on the wax.

3. Polish the surface with the soft cloth.

4. Rub some paint over the candle with a rag, making sure that it goes into all the hollows.

5. Leave this for a few minutes and then wipe it off with another rag, leaving the paint in the carved details.

6. Let the paint dry and then give the candle a final polish with the soft cloth.

Now experiment

Try carving figures of friends and relatives, making up a 'family' of candles. Use different sizes and shapes of candle for various types of design, and paint them in a variety of colours.

Balsa

Of all the many kinds of wood which can be carved, the softest is balsa, which comes from South America. It is very light and can be bought in most hobby supply stores.

Models and figures carved from balsa wood have a smooth, pleasing quality, both to look at and to touch.

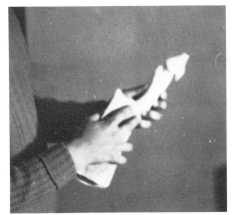

Collect
A block of balsa
Pencil
Penknife
Junior hacksaw
Rasp
Fine sandpaper
Varnish

How to start
1. Draw a design on the wood.
2. Saw off the biggest pieces with the hacksaw. (The photograph shows how to hold it.)
3. Continue shaping the wood with the penknife and rasp.
4. When the carving is completed, smooth it over with the sandpaper.
5. Give it a coat of varnish to protect it. More than one coat may be needed as it will soak into the wood a little.

Now experiment
Try carving a collection of animals of different species, varnishing some and painting on the details of others.

Carve a block of balsa to form a mount for one of your other carvings, one from soap, for instance.

Plywood

Plywood is laminated, which means it is made from thin layers of wood stuck together with the grain running in different directions. This makes it very strong and as the layers are sometimes

made from different coloured woods, they can be used to make interesting carvings.

Two animals carved from balsa. You can paint them or leave the wood plain.

Collect
A piece of 5-ply (plywood with five layers)
Pencil
Hacksaw
Fine rasp
Varnish
Sandpaper

How to start
1. Draw the outline of a design on the plywood.
2. Cut it out with the hacksaw. The wood will need to be placed in a clamp to hold it steady.
3. Now start to shape the edges with

An abstract carving in plywood. See how cleverly the layers of wood have been exposed to complement the shape of the carving. The different colours have been brought out with varnish.

the rasp, cutting across the wood so that all the layers are exposed.

4. Smooth the carving with sandpaper.

5. Mount it on a block of wood using nails or a wood glue.

6. Varnish it to bring out the colours of the different layers.

Whittling

'Whittling' is an Old English word meaning carving with a knife. It was often done by shepherds who would pick up bits of stick and make carvings as they watched their sheep. They would sell or exchange their work for goods when they went to market.

It is the simplest form of carving and while it needs little equipment, many fine objects are whittled by people all over the world. Africans and American Indians decorated their weapons in this way to great effect.

Collect
A stick
Penknife

How to start
Either cut away the bark on the stick or make use of it as part of the design. Use the natural shape of the stick to decide the carving — in this way less wood will need to be cut away and the design will be more satisfying. Hold the stick firmly and always cut away from the hand holding the work.

Work patiently, a little at a time, particularly with a small, thin piece of wood.

Make a collection of items such as a knife and fork, a set of bottle stoppers and a paper knife.

Driftwood

Collect
Pieces of interesting driftwood or twigs
Penknife
Fine rasp
Junior hacksaw
Sandpaper

Created entirely by nature, driftwood is a work of art in itself, and with careful carving and varnishing, you can make superb and unique ornaments with it. The best places to find driftwood are along the seashore at low tide or on the banks of a tidal river. Even if you are nowhere near the seashore or river bank, there are always interesting pieces of dry wood and twigs to be found in the open country, woods or parks. Never break twigs from a living tree and be sure to ask permission before taking anything from private ground.

How to start
1. Clean off any rotten wood or unwanted bark with the penknife.

2. Look at the piece of wood, turning it this way and that, until its shape suggests something specific – an animal or a head perhaps?
3. Decide what it is to represent, then work on it with the tools until it resembles the thing in mind as closely as possible.
4. Smooth the carving with sandpaper, then mount it and varnish it to give it a finished look.

The pictures on the previous pages show some examples of whittling (top, left); a traditional scrimshaw design of a sea scene scratched on bone (bottom, left). Right, the natural shape of the pieces of driftwood inspired these two dramatic carvings.

Bone scrimshaw

This is an ancient craft practised by different people throughout the world, carving various types of bone including the ivory tusks of the elephant and the walrus. The Eskimos have always carved whale bone and walrus tusks and very often they scratched designs on the ivory, rubbing black into the designs to make them stand out. The craft was taken up by the seamen in the old sailing ships and was called scrimshaw.

Ivory is not only hard to cut, but very expensive and many of the animals from which it comes are now in danger of extinction. Bone is softer and can be got quite cheaply from the butcher.

How to start
1. Clean the bone by boiling it for about an hour. Scrape off any pieces of meat or gristle left.
2. For a more finished look cut the ends

Collect
A bone
Junior hacksaw
Penknife
Rasp
Fine sandpaper
Black acrylic paint
Rag
Soft cloth

neatly with the hacksaw then smooth the edges with sandpaper.

3. Use a penknife to scratch a pattern on the bone's surface.

4. Rub black paint into the design, using a rag, then clean off the excess paint.

5. When it is completely dry, polish the finished scrimshaw with a soft cloth.

Maritime museums may display examples of scrimshaw which might provide some ideas.

Shell

The intricate designs and delicate colours of shells are fascinating and beautiful. Deeply carved shells — called cameos — are made for jewellery and ornaments and some very fine examples can be seen in certain museums. Try shaping some shells from the seashore in the same way.

Collect
Shells
Hacksaw
Fine rasp
Corn oil
Sandpaper
Bristle nailbrush
Penknife

How to start
1. Cut the edges of the shell carefully with the hacksaw to make an interesting shape.

2. Trim off any unwanted pieces with the rasp.

3. Sandpaper the shell to remove the chalky surface.

4. Use the knife to scratch in any details you wish to add.

5. To bring out the colour of the shell soak it for a while in corn oil.

6. Finally wash the shell in soap and water to remove the oil and then polish with the nailbrush.

Some examples of carved shells. They can be made into very attractive pendants by drilling a hole very carefully through the shell, near the edge, and hanging it on a long cord.

This piece of slate is a beautiful grey-green colour. The carving illustrates how slate can be cut in clean hard lines, or softer, rounded ones.

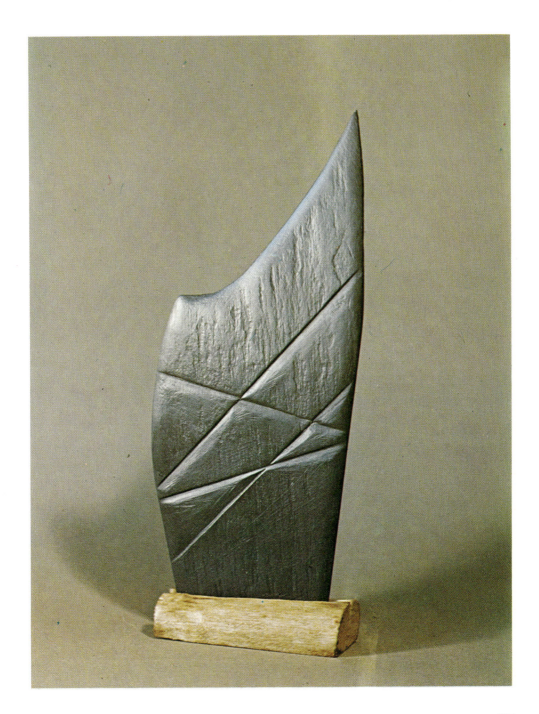

Slate

Slate is a fairly soft stone which has a definite character of its own. It was formed from mud which hardened over a million years ago and because of this it flakes off in layers very easily. It is easy to work, but you must treat it with care as it will break and chip very easily if you drop it or knock it hard.

In some parts of the country slate can be picked up from the ground, but if there is none near by, ask a builder for some broken roofing slates.

How to start
1. Draw a simple shape on the slate and cut it out with the hacksaw, holding the slate steady in a clamp.
2. Shape it with the rasp.
3. Scratch a simple design on the surface of the slate using a knife.
4. Smooth the surface and the edges with sandpaper.
5. Coat the slate with wax polish and then warm it in front of a fire or in the sun. This will make the wax soak into the stone and bring out the colour.
6. Polish with a soft cloth.

Mount the finished carving by cutting a slot or hole just large enough to hold it in place in a block of wood. Make sure the base of the mount is broad enough to keep the carving from toppling over.

Collect
Slate
Pencil
Penknife
Hacksaw
Rasp
Fine sandpaper
Wax polish
Soft cloth

Stone

Long before man discovered the use of metals, he quarried and carved stone, in the form of reliefs on the walls of caves and in the form of statues and figures, some of gigantic proportions, representing men, animals and gods.

Pictures of the great carved figures of Easter Island, which are among the largest ever executed by man, might provide some interesting ideas.

Collect
A lump of soft stone
Chalk
Hacksaw
Rasp

How to start
1. Use the chalk to draw the basic design on the block of stone. Remember that this carving will be three dimensional, which means you will be looking at it from all sides, unlike a picture on a piece of paper.
2. Use the hacksaw to remove the largest pieces from the carving. It will help if the stone is held firmly in a clamp.
3. Continue to shape the stone using the rasp, which will give the stone a good finish.

A large carving can be stood outside, as the rain will not damage it, but varnish will spoil the surface.

Some stone carvings made in imitation of primitive Easter Island statues.

A grotesque row of heads made by carving apples.

Apples

The early American settlers used apples not only to eat but also as a material for making carvings. This idea explains how it is done in such a way that the carved apples can be kept as ornaments without going bad.

Collect
A big red apple
Penknife
Varnish

How to start
1. Pare off part of the peel where you plan to make a face, saving the peel for use later.

2. Carve a face using the penknife. Make the nose and mouth very broad as they will shrink as the apple dries.

3. Cut slits for the eyes and slip bits of peel into them. Shape other pieces of peel for eyebrows, moustache, beard, etc. Just lay them in position and they will stick as the apple dries.

4. Place the apple on a radiator to dry or in a very low oven at 120°F (60°C) for one hour.

5. Finish the shrinking process in a warm place for a few days.

6. Mount the head on a scrap of wood or a painted cotton reel (thread spool) and then treat the head with a thin layer of varnish to preserve it.

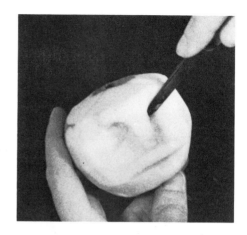

Now experiment

Once you have seen how the different carvings appear when they have shrunk, try making faces of friends or relatives and see how accurately you can make them.

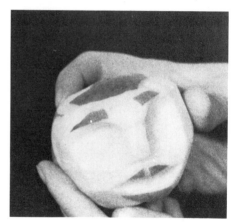

Totem poles

Finally, to end on a grand scale, try making a full-sized totem pole. Large cardboard boxes and packing cases are ideal, and it can be built as high as you can make it. Try using many of the techniques illustrated in this book.

You might get some ideas from looking at pictures of American Indian totem poles or Maori carvings and seeing how they were carved and painted.

Collect

Two large cardboard boxes or four smaller ones
Glue
Scissors
Powdered paints and brushes
Liquid dishwashing detergent
Coloured gummed paper
A collection of odds and ends such as cotton reels (thread spools), corks, bottle tops, seeds, foil, matchsticks, etc.

How to start

1. Glue the boxes together, one on top of the other.
2. Make a creamy mixture of powdered paint and liquid detergent. Four colours will do. Paint the boxes, each side in a different and contrasting colour.
3. Paint faces on each side of the boxes.
4. Add as much detail as possible by gluing on all the various odds and ends to represent such features as the eyes, mouth, teeth and nose, and painting them in bright colours.

Now experiment

Make the faces as different from each other as possible. Perhaps they could be humorous, or happy and sad alternately. You could make two faces look like animals or monsters and two look like people.

Try using different shaped boxes, beginning with a large one and ending with a small one at the very top. Spray the completed totem pole with gold or silver spray paint.

Many everyday materials can quite easily be carved into very satisfying shapes. Make a collection of as many different materials as possible, then try using the ideas in this book to transform them. Try using, for example, chocolate or beeswax, cuttlefish, or even orange peel, removing it from the orange carefully, all in one piece.

A totem pole.